W9-BGN-849

NIGHT MARKETS

NIGHT MARKETS

Bringing Food to a City   by Joshua Horwitz

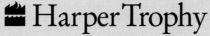

HarperTrophy

A Division of HarperCollinsPublishers

Special thanks to Sheryl Reich
for all her enthusiasm and bright ideas

Night Markets: Bringing Food to a City
Copyright © 1984 by Joshua Horwitz
Printed in the U.S.A. All rights reserved.

Library of Congress Cataloging in Publication Data
Horwitz, Joshua.
    Night markets.

    Summary: Text and photographs document the activities
at a variety of wholesale markets that supply meat, fish,
produce, baked goods, and dairy products to New York City.
    1. Produce trade—New York (N.Y.)—Juvenile literature.
2. New York (N.Y.)—Markets—Juvenile literature.
3. Wholesale trade—New York (N.Y.)—Juvenile literature.
4. Food supply—New York (N.Y.)—Juvenile literature.
[1. Food supply—New York (N.Y.)   2. Wholesale trade—
New York (N.Y.)   3. New York (N.Y.)—Markets.   4. Mar-
kets]   I. Title.
HD9008.N5H67   1984   381′.415′097471   83-45242
ISBN 0-690-04378-3
ISBN 0-690-04379-1 (lib. bdg.)
    "A Harper Trophy book"
ISBN 0-06-446046-0 (pbk.)   85-45401

Designed by Al Cetta
First Harper Trophy edition, 1986.
Published in hardcover by Thomas Y. Crowell, New York

To my mother

It's the middle of the night in New York City. A lot of lights are still on, but most of the seven million people who live here have gone to sleep. In a few hours they'll wake up to face another day in the big city—and they'll be hungry.

Hungry for their breakfast of bacon and eggs or bagels and lox. Later on they'll lunch on green salad with fresh fruit for dessert. And at dinner time they'll want a thick steak, or perhaps some fresh fish, on their tables. After all, they've had a hard day—they deserve it.

But where will all this food come from? Not much grows here, except skyscrapers. There are no cows grazing or corn stalks growing in Central Park. The fish are long gone from the rivers, gone in search of bluer waters.

All cities face the problem of gathering food. For a city the size of New York, it's a big problem. So every night, while the city sleeps, an army of people set to work, bringing food to the city. Tons of food—from across the country and around the world. The procession begins before midnight and continues till dawn.

After a week at sea, a huge freighter docks at a pier on the East River. Five million pounds of bananas and pineapples are crammed inside its hull.

At a rail spur in the Bronx, a boxcar full of broccoli and ice has completed its trip from California.

14

And out at the airport, crews are unloading a refrigerated freight plane packed with fruit and flowers from the Middle East.

The cargo is quickly sorted and transferred into waiting trucks, then rushed to market.

From nearby airports, piers, and train yards, from faraway farms and stockyards, remote fishing ports and dairies, trucks converge on the island of New York. By midnight, caravans of tractor-trailers are lined up at the bridges and tunnels leading into the city.

Across the river in Manhattan, beef trucks from the Midwest are backing up to one of the warehouses at the Gansevoort Meat Market.

Alongside are truckloads of chickens from
Maryland's "bird farms," rabbits from Georgia,

and all kinds of pork—ham, sausage, frankfurters,
pork chops, and whole suckling pigs.

At the Imperial Veal & Lamb Company, the veal calves arrive from the Nebraska slaughterhouse wrapped in cheesecloth. Since they weigh almost three hundred pounds, they are moved around on hooks and pulleys.

Hundreds of carcasses already hang by their hooves in the meat locker. Kept at a chilly 45° F., the meat locker resembles a huge refrigerator with bright lights and white walls. All the men who work inside have to wear hats and white coats. And they all carry sharp knives.

First, each carcass must be skinned. The pelt is removed in one large piece, then sold to make leather goods.

Next, a man with a blowtorch and brush makes sure the carcass is clean of any remaining hair or bristles.

Now the calf is ready to be sectioned and carved into shoulder, rib, and loin cuts.

At another counter they fillet the veal into cutlets.
Out back the local butcher picks up his daily
order. By now the veal is light enough to be loaded
by hand.

On the other side of town, in the Bronx, the trucks are streaming in and out of the Terminal Market at Hunts Point. Hunts Point consists of 125 acres of trucks, boxcars, and loading docks. Two billion pounds of fresh fruit and vegetables are sold here each year, making it the largest produce market in the world. That's enough produce to fill a baseball stadium ten times over.

The produce comes by plane, train, boat, and truck, from as far away as Israel. Florida oranges take three days to arrive by truck. A trainload of strawberries from California makes the trip in about a week. Most of the fruit is picked early, then allowed to ripen on the way to market. Once there it is sold as quickly as possible, before it can spoil.

You don't come to Hunts Point to buy a few
apples or tomatoes. Peek inside the warehouses
and you'll find a mountain of onions, or a sea of
watermelons.

The truckloads are broken down into bushels and pecks, cases and crates. Then the produce is sold to supermarkets, greengrocers, and restaurants.

If there's going to be fresh bread in the morning, someone has to get up early to bake it. On East 14th Street, they start making bialys at 3 A.M. Named after the Polish city of Bialystok where they were first baked, bialys look like a cross between a roll and a bagel.

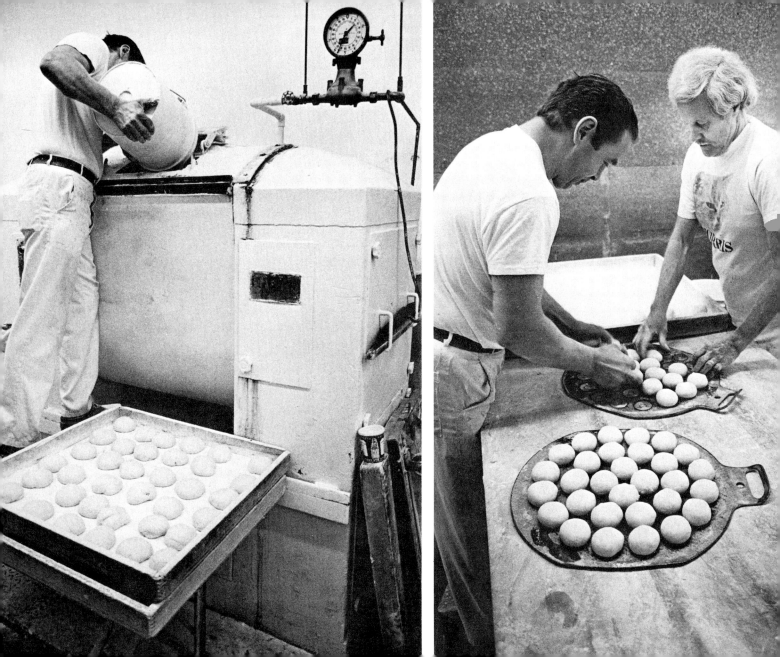

Vast quantities of water, flour, salt, and yeast are mixed together in a large dough vat. Another machine presses the dough into balls, which are placed in flour-lined trays.

This three-man operation functions like a well-oiled assembly line. While the oven is heating up, two men press the balls with their thumbs to create the distinctive dimpled shape.

The third man smears each bialy with onion paste.

48

When the oven reaches 800° F., the baking begins. Two men lay the bialys in neat rows on long-handled wood pallets. The other loads the oven, sliding the bialys smoothly off the pallets with a twist of the wrist. The oven has five revolving tiers, so the loading must continue at a fast clip to ensure even baking.

Seven minutes later the process is reversed—and out come the first of the 1200 dozen bialys they will bake by dawn. Scores of restaurants and groceries are depending on them.

Of course you can't eat a rose, but flowers are as much a staple of urban life as bread and apples. A splash of color against a gray concrete landscape. A breath of fresh air amidst the exhaust fumes. In a hundred small ways, flowers provide nourishment for the city dweller.

The wholesale flower district covers twelve blocks of midtown Manhattan and is as lively as any of the night markets in New York City. Before the morning rush hour begins and the customers start to arrive, the flowers must be unpacked and set out on sidewalks or arranged on counters.

Potted plants can live and grow in the store, but cut flowers are highly perishable and must be flown in daily aboard refrigerated jets. They arrive packed in ice—orchids from Hawaii, poinsettias from Florida.

Crates of roses and carnations, boxes of chrysanthemums and daisies are unpacked, arranged in bouquets, or laid out in massive piles on tables. There are hundreds of floral shops in New York.

Before dawn the florists arrive and examine the day's offerings. They are careful to choose the flowers with the tightest buds and greenest stems. Like the greengrocers, they can't afford to be stuck with spoiled goods.

The flower district smells like a rose, but there's a stronger scent in the air downtown on the waterfront. You can smell the fish for six blocks around the Fulton Fish Market. It is New York's oldest market, dating back to the 18th century, and the largest fish outlet in the country. Every year 175 million pounds of fish move through here. Laid end to end, they would stretch from New York to Los Angeles and back.

Fish lie about everywhere—on the pavement, on
tables, in buckets and boxes. Big fish, little fish,
and shellfish. Some of the fish are caught in
nearby waters, but most are trucked in from all

over the eastern seaboard—red snapper from Florida, scrod and bluefish from Massachusetts, swordfish and pompano from the Carolinas. Twice a week there are salmon flown in from fish farms in Norway.

When it comes to picking fish, freshness is the key. Everything arrives packed in ice, but you never know how long the fishing boat was out at sea or which truck might have had a breakdown along the way. So you have to make your selections carefully. A fresh fish should have bright, clear eyes, good color and smell, and firm flesh with tight, shiny skin. If you're a restaurant chef buying your special "catch of the day," you have to do a lot of looking, touching, and sniffing before you make your choice.

Through the night a lot of swordfish get cut into steaks, and countless bucketfuls of squid and smelts are weighed and sold.

70

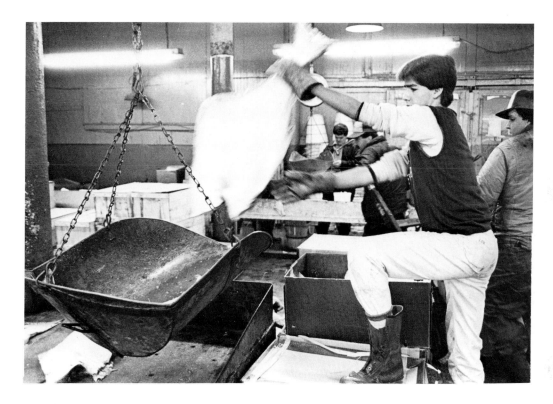

Sushi chefs haggle over the best fillets,
while retail fishmongers keep track of the latest
price-per-pound quotations.

They're already packing up the vans and hosing down the stalls by the time the sun rises over the Brooklyn Bridge.

It's just after dawn, but some New Yorkers are already out working up an appetite.

Downtown in the dairy district, they're still
unloading butter and eggs...

...while around the corner at the Market Diner, the kitchen prepares for the breakfast rush.

Meanwhile, the commuters are streaming back into the city. On their way to offices, they pause for a cup of coffee...

a piece of fruit...

or a morning pastry.

In other parts of town, people in less of a hurry are sitting down to hearty breakfasts at fancy restaurants...

or enjoying some sun and the morning newspaper
at home.

As New Yorkers begin the day with full stomachs, the empty trucks head out of town. Tonight they will return to link the city with the world's food chain.

Meanwhile, on a hi-rise terrace overlooking the big city, a small tomato crop gets some personal attention—just in case the trucks break down.